1 9 2 9 ˴ 1 9 9 4

"She will be remembered as the American woman at her best: brave, disciplined, ironical, imperturbable, filled with a vivid sense of the potentiality and the sadness of life."

—ARTHUR SCHLESINGER, JR.

Uncommon Grace

Reminiscences and Photographs of
Jacqueline Bouvier Kennedy Onassis

J.C. Suarès

J. Spencer Beck

Introduction by Nina Auchincloss Straight

THOMASSON-GRANT

Charlottesville, Virginia

The authors would like to gratefully acknowledge the help of Khoi Nguyen for his chapter introductions and his invaluable assistance throughout the project.

Published by
Thomasson-Grant, Inc.

Copyright © 1994
J.C. Suarès.
Text copyright ©
J. Spencer Beck.
Editorial Director:
Susie Shulman.
Photo Editor: Leslie Fratkin.

ISBN 1-56566-077-3

FRONT COVER AND PAGE 19: Taking a break from her husband's hectic campaign for the Presidential nomination, Jacqueline Kennedy relaxed in Hyannis Port during the summer of 1959.

BACK COVER: Even after remarrying in 1968, Jacqueline Onassis still sought solace by the sea at the Kennedy compound in Hyannis Port.

PAGE 1: The wife of Senator John Kennedy posed for a formal portrait by photographer Yousuf Karsh in 1957.

PAGE 2: The new First Lady attended the Piedmont Hunt Point-to-Point races in Upperville, Virginia, in March of 1961.

Photography Credits:

CONTENTS

UNCOMMON GRACE

J. C. SUARÈS

othing I'd heard or read about her prepared me for the actual face-to-face meeting. Some people amount to a lot less than the sum of their parts. Others turn out to be just ordinary people like you and me. A few rise above even the greatest expectations. She was one of the latter; she exuded such grace, charm, and intelligence that she left everyone who crossed her path to wonder if she had come from another world.

In 1984, the most famous woman in the world, Jacqueline Kennedy Onassis, then an editor at Doubleday, the prestigious (and still family-owned) New York publishing house, agreed to edit and even write a brief envoi to a book by Michael Jackson—the pop music icon of the decade. Jackson's "Thriller" album had enjoyed stratospheric success. By 1984, it had sold over 40 million copies—almost twice as many as any other album in history.

The book was slated for fall of 1986 and was to be a large-format, coffee-table extravaganza. Michael asked Robert Hilburn, the *Los Angeles Times* pop music critic he had met in 1970, to write the text. I was contracted to art direct the book, titled *Moonwalk*. My job was to accompany Jackie to Michael's Encino, California, home and work with her and the singer to orchestrate the marriage of text and photographs from Jackson's huge archive and to set up new shots of the star's paraphernalia—gloves, awards, costumes, et cetera.

Jackie could not have been thrilled with the prospect of editing the book. For one thing, it meant that she would have to make at least three trips to L.A., spending several days at a time

The most photographed woman in the world almost never posed for the camera, but she did during this 1985
working meeting with pop superstar Michael Jackson, whose autobiography, Moonwalk, she was editing for Doubleday.

away from her beloved homes in New York and New Jersey. For another, she had not the least interest in Michael's music. A book about Versailles, Russian costumes, or ballet would have been much more her cup of tea.

But Jackie was a trooper, and she knew full well that without her involvement, Doubleday would not have acquired the book for less than seven figures. She was also driven by a certain curiosity about the man who was even more inscrutable than she—Michael Jackson—and she knew that she was embarking on a strange adventure to La-La Land. What she didn't anticipate was that getting a real book out of him—one in which he would share his innermost thoughts about serious matters such as his family troubles, his alleged fixations on children and pets, and his sexual ambiguity—would prove out of the question. So secretive was he that just prior to our beginning work, Michael had arranged for a press conference at which his manager, Frank Dileo, read a statement warning that Jackson would sue any publication that spread false accusations about the star's personal life.

Compared with her customary environment— an understated, classically furnished Fifth Avenue apartment with a magnificent view of Central Park— Michael's Encino compound must have seemed to her a kitsch palace. One can only imagine how her refined sensibilities were affected by the excesses and carnivallike atmosphere of the main house, with its massive living room decorated with great crystal chandeliers and paintings of clowns; the trophy room, boasting a dozen display cases filled with Michael's music and video awards; the "macrobiotic-only" kitchen, manned by a Sikh-costumed chef (turban and all); several playrooms housing the indoor menagerie including "Muscles" the boa constrictor; and Michael's two-tiered bedroom complete with a number of male and female mannequins placed strategically throughout like silent roommates.

Connected to the kitchen was the dining room, in which a long table for ten sat seldom used. This room would become our office, where Jackie and her assistant, Shaye Areheart, would edit the manuscript, I would design the pages, and Michael would eat popcorn and drink from a large bottle of Evian.

The estate seemed unusually quiet for a rock star's domain. There was no central sound system, no multimedia gadgetry. Even the occasional two or three fans at the gate kept silent vigil under the watchful eye of the chief of security and his staff. Jackie took in the whole scene with characteristic grace. She felt sorry for the lonely animals and was puzzled by the mannequins, but did not voice these sentiments until later, over lunch at the Beverly Hills Hotel.

For Jackie, the biggest mystery revolved around Michael's sexuality. He revealed nothing: there were no pictures in his bedroom, no hint of significant others except for a distant date with Brooke Shields. "Do you think he likes girls?" she'd ask, at least once a day. She hadn't a clue, and the star's ambiguity only made her more curious.

The first draft of the manuscript arrived in the spring of 1985, and it was immediately clear to Jackie that it wasn't going to work. Tantamount to a giant press release, it was all puff and no substance. Michael had refused to speak candidly or impart any real truths about himself; instead, his ramblings sounded like a casual telephone conversation with a fan: "It's hard for me to say which is my favorite song of the songs I've written . . . but 'Heartbreak Hotel' is the most personal." And so on.

That was it. No more, no less. After much deliberation, Jackie decided to reject the manuscript, but she didn't want to upset Michael. She gave him an ultimatum in a calm, firm voice. She instructed him to open up and give the reader a sincere show of feeling—about growing up Black in show business, for example. "There must be some good guys and bad guys," she urged. Then she concluded by telling him that if the book was all fluff, "we'd all be made fools of."

Jackie seemed proud of her tough but understated performance. I likened it to vintage Bette Davis. She loved the comparison so much that she called me a few days later to ask if I'd really meant it.

For comic relief amid the stress of working long days in Encino, we treated ourselves to lavish lunches in L.A. One such lunch was at Ma Maison. I invited publishing maven Martha Stewart, who happened to be in town that week, to join us. Incredibly, Martha arrived an hour late, but quickly disarmed Jackie with her charm. Although she appreciated Martha's style, Jackie did not quite understand how it had become an entire industry: she assumed that most people knew how to arrange roses and polish old silver and that those who didn't had gardeners and maids who did. After that day, she could never remember Martha's name and always referred to her as "that pretty girl." I don't think they ever spoke again.

As for the manuscript, Michael worked with Hilburn, following Jackie's carefully prescribed outline. But he wrote without emotion. He spoke flatly of his difficult early years in Gary, Indiana, where he grew up in a large family ruled by a tyrannical father. He described the much-publicized break between the Jacksons and Motown Records as if he were reading a news dispatch. He talked about practicing his craft—songwriting, singing, dancing, performing before huge audiences—as if it were the most natural thing in the world. The monotone of his voice as it came through in the writing begged the question: Had he achieved the pinnacle of the music profession without the slightest

angst, self-doubt, or artistic struggle?

A good bit of the manuscript dealt with his show-biz acquaintances—presented as a kind of mutual admiration society. Here was Fred Astaire telling Michael what a great dancer he was, and Michael telling Elizabeth Taylor how much he admired her, and Katharine Hepburn telling Michael what a great star he was, and the great star telling Diana Ross how he loved her.

About his sexuality, which had so intrigued Jackie, he would offer only: "My dating and relationships with girls have not had the happy endings I've been looking for. Something always seems to get in the way." On the plane ride back to New York, Jackie predicted that he would marry a child-woman at thirty-five. She was almost right.

In the end, the book was rewritten, postponed, postponed again, and eventually published in 1988—two years late and in a much more spartan package than originally envisioned. It enjoyed a short-lived, modest success.

Jackie looked back on the whole experience as one of the more fascinating chapters in her career as an editor. We went on to work together on four more books—all lavishly illustrated coffee-table albums, which she loved. At the end of each project, she'd send a personal note. The first one was typewritten on Doubleday letterhead, but the later ones were handwritten on her personal stationery. Each gracious note conveyed her thanks to me as an equal partner in the making of the book. In the end what mattered to her was that there had been a maximum of integrity, no compromises, and no gimmicks.

Was she from another world, or another era? Perhaps. But the lessons we learned from her serve us well in ours—and for all time.

A FAMILY ALBUM

NINA AUCHINCLOSS STRAIGHT

Her looks were not an acquired taste. The symmetry of her face was obvious to anyone. The large hazel eyes, set far apart, never needed any shadow or liner, as the lashes were nearly black, as were her eyebrows. Her mouth was large, curved in a bold balance, and her nose, small and neat, never had an awkward angle on camera. The elements of her face, framed by her brown and wavy hair, were striking, and the camera loved them. She almost never took a bad photograph, with the possible exception of a few baby pictures, when she had no hair, and a series of photographs announcing her engagement to Senator John Fitzgerald Kennedy for the cover of *LIFE* in July 1953, where she is profiled on the sea-splashed deck of a heeling sailboat. If a person's ideal is a Memling Madonna or a Gauguin Tahitian, then perhaps they might not have considered her beautiful. Certainly, "no one looked like her," as Senator Edward M. Kennedy remarked in his eulogy on May 23, 1994, in memory of Jacqueline Lee Bouvier Kennedy Onassis.

She had the body of a dancer, although she couldn't dance. She had a long, slim torso, and the curves in her arms appeared to have been chiseled. Her good posture was more of an equestrian's sense of balance through the shoulders and the heel of the foot than that of a ballerina. Yet she adored the ballet, the ultimate *tableau vivant*.

She was born to be seen in modern times. She did not need formality in order to look elegant. It was impossible for her to look sloppy, even deplaning in Washington after the events in Dallas. Growing up, she went through no awkward stages. She starred in most styles of the Twentieth Century, starting with the padded shoulders, horizontally tucked or draped skirts, and

A "Merrywood" Merry Christmas, McLean, Virginia, 1951: Lee and Jackie (Bouvier),
Janet, Nina, Yusha, Jamie, and Tommy Auchincloss.

Coming out in style in 1947 meant the right tea dress, above, and a convertible Mercury (in Newport with sister Lee), right.

sling-back, open-toed shoes of the 1940s. She looked lovely in photographs, and she loved photography. It was her sense of destiny.

Scrapbooks were introduced into my life—I was the middle child of seven assorted children strung together into the third family of my father, Hugh Dudley Auchincloss—by Jackie's mother, my stepmother, Janet Norton Lee Bouvier Auchincloss. Aunt Janet's life's efforts, sailing over oxers and cavallettis to win hunter championships in Madison Square Garden, had been distilled like an Elizabethan "progress" into newsclips, society columns, and hundreds of snapshots, which were pasted into photo albums whose layouts looked like a combination of those in *Silver Screen* and *Vogue* magazines.

Jackie and Caroline Lee Bouvier (her younger sister, Lee) came to live with us in 1942, and both girls brought their own sets of scrapbooks. I spent hours with their handiwork. It was like reading other people's mail. Pictures of themselves were captioned "Me" (initials were for third persons—non-family members) and then pasted in a format for instant immortality. Those of us who appeared less than sublime on Kodak or Ansco's celluloid film, unloved by the lens of a Brownie Reflex or Speed Graphic, took up hiding, then painting, poetry, or prose.

Putting together a scrapbook develops the editorial eye, how to look at things for a purpose, a design.

Art history was my stepmother's favorite academic and artistic enthusiasm. She adored John Walker, head of the National Gallery of Art. We all trooped through museums, looked at art books, "L'art et la Mode," the collected mannerisms of the great French courtesans, and studied ballet books of the Paris Opera for composition and line. By looking at yourself and other people you learn how to be looked at.

"Pasting" is a form of editing in the assembling of photo albums: it is the colorful pamphleteering of one's version of family members and family life. The house *on dit* was that we were always supposed to make, not buy, the presents we gave. So, we produced and presented photo albums and scrapbooks as offerings to our parents on anniversaries, birthdays, and holidays. Any family event could also result in a picture book. Jackie sketched "The Red Shoes," in honor of our youngest sister, Janet Jennings Auchincloss. Another album was dedicated to our old show mare, "Danseuse." *One Special Summer*, compiled by Jackie and Lee during a European trip in 1951, was even published by a real publishing house and people purchased it out in the real world.

If the Brontë sisters all wrote, we all pasted. And when we weren't all pasting or by ourselves engaged in singular pursuits, the girls from Hammersmith Farm, my father's summer house in Newport, Rhode Island, were out taking pictures or being photographed with our dog, car, birthday cake, or under the Christmas tree for another group holiday photo. Jackie was a natural at her first

The future Inquiring Photographer for the Washington Times-Herald *practices on sister Lee in 1951.*

job, as the Inquiring Photographer for the *Washington Times-Herald*. On a slow news day, the family and our friends, done up in a variety of weird disguises, were enlisted for photographs and then quizzed for quotes to fill out her columns—just like another scrapbook.

On one particular school holiday, Jackie cornered me and my cohorts as we taped our own "radio show," complete with guitars, advertisements, and melodrama. The grand production number, a solo by C. D. B. Bryan, who went on to write *Friendly Fire* and win a National Book Award, screeched to a halt as budding journalist Jackie inquired, "Do you suppose . . .?" The question concerned John Locke's maxim about a "sound mind" and a "sound body." For a fifties teenager to discuss her thoughts on "body" in mixed company—and for publication to boot—was true mortification indeed. One of our guitarists, a physicist now living in Portola Valley, California, wrote and asked me years later if I remembered our days in the "Inquiring Photographer" columns. Who could forget?

The driving force in our lives during these years was my Aunt Janet, Jackie's mother. My only mothering parent, really, she was occasionally assisted by Jackie, who, when I was younger, had translated my French lectures so I could stay outdoors until dark (that is, until Mlle. Gabby at the Potomac School for Girls suspected my new-found fluency in her native tongue was more

Jackie's than mine). Jackie's favorite description of her mother belonged to a man; he described Aunt Janet's entrance into a room as "a breath of fresh air." Fastidiously feminine, she loved animals, countrysides, tending to abandoned children as a nurse's aide in a Washington, D.C., hospital, society black-tie dinners almost every night of the week, and living out everyone's childhood, making their wishes come true, as when she once roamed the countryside far and wide to buy me my first pet, a dog.

Almost unique among women of any era, Aunt Janet believed in being born a girl. Being a boy, growing up to be a man, had absolutely nothing to do with our childhood household. Her mother's pride and joy, if not her actual favorite, Jackie possessed a "sense of self" fortified by her mother's family circle, and in return Jackie fortified everyone else's idea of family with her own sense of occasion—"what's to be done." Black Jack Bouvier had enhanced Jackie's early sophisticated sense of self. But she always thought a woman could not go far if she could not "go home." And for her mother's last years, when Aunt Janet was bewildered by Alzheimer's, Jackie subsidized her home, organizing and arranging down to the last detail her personal effects, the staff, surroundings and daily routines—all of which enabled Aunt Janet to sail through those later years with a smile.

Aunt Janet's power in our lives was pervasive. Some of us married. Some of us were married off. Lee married Michael Canfield in the spring of 1953. Theater, front and center, would be more amusing, Jackie

After the writer's 1957 marriage to Newton Ivan Steers, matron-of-honor Jackie greets
Senator Theodore Green of Rhode Island, while youngest sister Janet mugs for the camera.

thought, than booklets passed out among wedding guests. So Jackie wrote for the two of us an in-house dialogue for the event and sent it up to me at boarding school. The subject was marital wallflowerdom—why no one had proposed to us. Casting us both as a little too horsey in aroma and me in my real-life role as her Sancho Panza, Jackie had me ask the question: "Well, Jack 'ole Hack—what do you think the future holds for us?" Jackie was to suggest that we offer ourselves up as "maids," because Michael and Lee would be giving many dinner parties, entertaining "New York's brilliant young married set," and, by waiting on tables, we could introduce ourselves to "all of New York's eligible bachelors." Besides, Jackie scripted herself as realistically pointing out that the cheapest wedding present we could give would be "ourselves." Divine intervention made my train late to arrive from Miss Porter's. . . . In September 1953, Jackie married John Kennedy.

Even after her marriage, Jackie returned home. When Jack Kennedy was not traveling, they frequently lived at Merrywood, my father's winter house in McLean, Virginia. True, they had rented houses, but the Senate sessions did not always coincide with the leases. Then they bought Hickory Hill house in Virginia. But after Jack's last-minute bid for the vice presidency in August of 1956, Jackie returned to summer at Hammersmith Farm. There she lost baby Arabella. Bobby and Ethel Kennedy soon bought Hickory Hill, since Jackie felt a bit isolated in Virginia. Eventually, she and Jack moved to N Street in Georgetown. But it was never unusual over summer weekends in the fifties to find the five top bedrooms on the third floor of Hammersmith Farm, a bit like *Little Women* revisited, filled with my half-brother, Yusha, Jackie and Jack, Lee and Mike, myself, and then, eventually, my first husband, Newton Ivan Steers. The fifth room was for clothes. The outside bedroom doors were louvered for sea breezes, so the top of the house lilted with conversations, secrets, and laughter—rather like a cocktail party. Jackie returned home with Caroline and John-

John to Hammersmith the summer after the assassination in 1963. In a few years, her lifelong friend, Nancy Tuckerman—"Tucky"—would relay to the world that Mrs. Auchincloss had announced Jackie's marriage to Aristotle Onassis.

Even if society columnist Cholly Knickerbocker had not had Jacqueline Bouvier photographed in 1947 as "Debutante of the Year," her *rites du progrès*, like her mother's, would have been recorded in family scrapbooks. Earlier that same year, an unknown photographer had snapped Jackie in coming-out white, profiled by a mantelpiece, in an at-home rendition of Mme. Gautreau, popularly known as "X."

Just after becoming Mrs. Kennedy, she was photographed by Toni Frissell at the wedding, later on by Yousuf Karsh. It was more destiny than irony that she married men, both times, who created publicity and who loved to be photographed. As Philip B. Kundhardt, Jr., wrote in *Life in Camelot*: "John F. Kennedy was the first president to realize what powerful allies photographs could be."

Some people can say they did what they wanted to do in life. Others can say they did what they set out to do. But few people can claim to have truly lived life the way they wanted to. Jackie insisted. The August 1994 issue of *Vogue* republished her Prix de Paris–winning essays circa 1951. Like her photograph in that issue, they are a clear-eyed, steady statement, a disarmingly bold, accurate, and astute account of herself for all time. Her format did not change over the years; it varied like a classical ballet, deepening melodically to encompass the sometimes horrible, historic themes of her marriages, her love of Jack, her necessity for Onassis, and her endless personal curiosity about her family circle, which eventually grew to include her children, grandchildren, and all of her maternal nieces and nephews in varying degrees.

Her choreography stayed the course. It was an extraordinary life that consciously came full circle: a work of art, crafted with the help of Tucky and, later, Maurice Tempelsman, who had been part of her inner circle during her public as well as private life. He was a man who protected her time to remember "happy" memories.

One of the many bedrooms in which I was bivouacked as a child was Jackie's luminous room facing west at Hammersmith Farm. Just after she had built her house across the Gay Head border, in Martha's Vineyard, she took me up to see her bedroom. She was grinning. What did it remind me of? She had unconsciously duplicated the crazy shape and sequence—if not the actual size and number—of the Victorian windows in our Hammersmith bedroom. Memories.

Jackie's christening, her confirmation, and her funeral mass were all held in Manhattan's St. Ignatius Loyola church. In his eulogy, Senator Kennedy pointed up Jacqueline's "unique sense of self." It was a sensibility best described as "artistic" in that it was her own "version" of things. Sometimes it was caught in her caricatures—simple, yet detailed, intimately funny pen, ink, and watercolor sketches of family and friends. But her singular view of life could best be seen in a photograph. Pictures were about being beautiful, brave; they were about family relations and friends. Her photograph of choice would have been the kind selected for a postcard: What to *look* like in life. Jackie knew what kind of a "postcard" she wanted to send, as well as what message she wanted to deliver on the flip side. For a first choice, the postcard of herself and three sisters would have been the inevitable photograph used in all English fox-hunting histories of the Melton and the fearsome Leicestershire countryside: the "Four Cadogan Daughters of Viscount Chelsea" in their black sidesaddle habits, derbies, and veils. Growing up, much of the time we were just three girls. More artistically profound, another version would have been a painting, reproduced for the Metropolitan Museum of Art's card series, "Women in White." A

favorite of Jackie's from this series was John Singer Sargent's 1899 oil of the three Wyndham sisters—even if Mrs. Tennant *was* toppling off the sofa's backrest.

A variation on her mother's "breath of fresh air," Jackie was about living young. As late as the 1980s, on a dark and stormy Martha's Vineyard night, we snuck into a movie theater on our hands and knees to dry off and catch the last half hour of *An Officer and a Gentleman*. It was an encore of stunts we had pulled in the early 1950s, like the time we disembarked from a train with our hats and coats on backwards in order to (1) see who would notice and (2) see if we could get away with it. Happily, these remain forever photographs of the mind.

As a child and as an adult, Jacqueline Lee Bouvier Kennedy Onassis was a photographer, the subject of photographs, and an editor of picture books. We were all encouraged by the third Mrs. Hugh Dudley Auchincloss to follow her example and keep, not daily diaries, but voluminous scrapbooks. (I did several on my father's herd of lemon-and-white Guernseys that no one has ever looked at, including the cows.) My stepmother said that such books and albums should be religiously maintained in the present because it would be fun in the future to turn back pages and look at the past.

Jackie "rode to the hounds" until the last Thanksgiving of her life, November 1993. And during the times I hooked up with her and hunted foxes in Virginia's Piedmont, we sometimes talked about the past. She occasionally described her life, all of the stark tragedies and triumphs, as "a bit like a lunar roller coaster ride." Neither discursive nor argumentative, but always conclusive, she felt that "in the end, all you really have are happy memories."

You seemed immortal, as if fate arranged
That since the sixties you remain unchanged;
Superb in mourning, you became sublime:
Our silent icon, strangely fixed in time.
And still in all we cannot help but trace
The way you lived with such uncommon grace.

—CHRISTOPHER MASON

She was born on July 28, 1929, into a milieu that could not have been more auspicious for her parents, the John V. Bouvier IIIs. It was a few months before the Big Crash, and her "drippingly handsome" father and vivacious young mother made quite a pair attending society events in New York and summering in East Hampton, where her grandfather Bouvier's house, Lasata, was one of the showplaces of Long Island's East End.

Reared on Park Avenue, Jacqueline grew up believing the myth perpetuated by *Our Forebears*, a largely fabricated family history compiled by Jackie's grandfather, "the Major," that purported that the Bouviers were descended from a princely house of Savoy, in France. (In fact, the family's American progenitor, Michel Bouvier, was a cabinetmaker who emigrated from Provence to the United States in 1815.) Her mother, Janet Lee, also boasted of ancestral grandeur, proclaiming that she was one of "the Maryland Lees." Yet the truth was simple enough. The wealth of both the Lees, who were Irish and from New York, and the Bouviers, though estimable at times, was more recent than all of that. Perhaps that was why Janet so assiduously molded Jackie to fit into the role of a "lady." These early drills would one day allow the world's most famous woman to compose herself in any situation: she was perennially correct, unflappable.

"Black Jack" Bouvier, Jackie's father, on the other hand, doted on her as though she were a veritable princess. That only made things worse when, in 1940, at age eleven, she witnessed her parents' acrimonious divorce—caused as much by her father's financial irresponsibility as his much-gossiped-about womanizing. She forgave him these transgressions, and in fact paraded the Clark Gable look-alike at school events, where her friends would swoon. Years later, Jackie would confess that she found her handsome, debonair—if somewhat louche—father "a quite devastating figure."

Gliding swiftly on to her second marriage, to wealthy and eminently more respectable Hugh Dudley Auchincloss, Jr., of Virginia and Newport, Janet then more than ever ensured that Jackie and her younger sister, Lee—both of whom were thrust into ultra-proper, old-guard society—possessed the appearance and trappings of quintessential society girls. In the face of such intensive grooming, and still suffering the heartache of her parents' divorce, the sensitive Jackie turned inward, steeling herself with a self-possession that then—as later—would contribute to her much-discussed mystique.

Nevertheless, Jackie's inborn sense of leadership always managed to peek through the introverted facade. In 1947 she made her debut, and, thanks to her impeccable comportment, caught the discerning eye of Igor "Cholly Knickerbocker" Cassini. The era's reigning society columnist, Cassini anointed her "Debutante of the Year." Four years later, she won a prestigious writing contest sponsored by *Vogue* magazine. By then, young Jacqueline Bouvier had secured her footing in the columns that would one day chart her every move.

After two years at "that dreadful Vassar" and a junior year in Paris at the Sorbonne, Jackie finished her college education in Washington, D.C., at George Washington University. Upon graduation, she took a $42.50-a-week job as the Inquiring Photographer for the *Washington Times-Herald*. A daring and mischievous bachelorette, she often used her newspaper column as a forum for flirtation. She once even posed to an unsuspecting subject the question: "What's your idea of the perfect mate?"

In 1952, Jacqueline Bouvier thought she had found the perfect husband in the larger-than-life John Fitzgerald Kennedy, a figure who, in spite of his lofty aims, evoked, eerily, many of her father's traits. Luckily, the rigorous grounding in practicality she inherited from her mother—coupled with her father's style and flair—would prepare her well to withstand the vicissitudes attendant to a life lived under the harsh glare of the spotlight.

Mr. and Mrs. John Vernou Bouvier, III, of New York and East Hampton, escort five-year-old Jacqueline to the Southampton Horse Show in August of 1934. A champion equestrienne, Janet Lee Bouvier would pass on her love of riding— and her good horse sense—to her daughter.

RIGHT AND OPPOSITE PAGE: *Jacqueline Lee Bouvier was three-and-a-half when sister Caroline Lee ("Lee") was born in 1933. Strikingly dissimilar—Jackie's dark Bouvier looks and boisterous temperament contrasted with Lee's daintier features and polite disposition—both sisters would take an active interest in the Bouvier family menagerie, which eventually included six thoroughbred horses, three pedigreed dogs, and a pet rabbit Jackie kept in her bathtub. In 1935, they presented their White Bull Terrier, "Regent," opposite, at the annual East Hampton Dog Show.*

RIGHT: *Janet Norton Lee Bouvier, the daughter of a self-made millionaire, knew the value of a little publicity. Her elder daughter's fourth birthday party at Rowdy Hall, the Bouvier's summer rental in East Hampton, was duly noted by the society columnist for the East Hampton Star. The girl who would grow up to be the most famous woman in the world had already made her debut in print two years earlier for being a "charming hostess" at her second birthday celebration.*

RIGHT: *Bright, but high-strung and difficult to manage, Jackie also had a "fierce competitive edge," according to Queenie Simmonds-Nielson, the daughter of her riding master at the East Hampton Riding Club. In 1938, she won first prize dressed as an Indian at the club's annual costume contest.*

OPPOSITE PAGE AND FOLLOWING PAGES: *Her parents' bitter 1940 divorce and her mother's subsequent remarriage to the very rich and very WASPy Hugh Dudley Auchincloss, Jr., may have caused Jackie a good deal of heartache, but it also steeled her and fueled her innate rebelliousness. She went through the de rigueur motions of "coming out" in 1947, but "she never really took it seriously. It was a lark," remembers a childhood friend. Wearing a $59 off-the-rack gown (page 27), the strikingly self-possessed and unusual seventeen-year-old beauty was named Debutante of the Year anyway.*

OPPOSITE PAGE: *The woman who would spend most of her life hounded by photographers took a $42.50-a-week job as the Inquiring Photographer for the Washington Times-Herald after graduating as a transfer student from George Washington University in 1951. Pestering strangers with questions such as "Noel Coward once said, 'Women should be struck regularly, like gongs.' Do you agree?" Jackie flirted and then fell in love with one of her more interesting subjects—Senator John Fitzgerald Kennedy.*

ABOVE: *In August of 1949, a twenty-year-old Jacqueline Bouvier set sail from New York aboard the "De Grasse" for a year of study at the Sorbonne in Paris. Later describing her time in France as "the high point of my life, my happiest and most carefree year," the Vassar junior still had to write her mother each week, "or she gets hysterical and thinks I'm dead or married to an Italian." Although her ancestry was more Irish and English than French (her father, Black Jack, was only one-quarter French himself), Jackie would later capitalize on her Bouvier name and command of the French language to captivate Charles de Gaulle and millions of Frenchmen during her legendary trip to Paris with President Kennedy in 1961.*

Many saw it as the beginning of a wondrous journey, others as the first step down a thorny path. When, on September 12, 1953, Jacqueline Lee Bouvier exchanged vows with John Fitzgerald Kennedy in Newport's St. Mary's Church, she was nothing if not guileless at twenty-four.

He was thirty-six—the brilliant, ambitious Democratic senator who had long set his sights on the Presidency, the son of multimillionaire Joseph P. Kennedy, kingpin of America's ascendant political dynasty and former Ambassador to the Court of St. James.

That she was a rather impecunious child of divorced parents (her father had by then squandered much of his money on "wine, women, and song") did not mean that she was marrying up. Her mother had become a redoubtable grande dame of society as the third Mrs. Auchincloss, and the myth of the Bouvier's blue-blooded pedigree had yet to be challenged. Indeed, the union, if not for the unconditional love and loyalty Jackie devoted to her husband and his boisterous family, might well have been nothing more than a strategic merger overseen by the wily ambassador to forge an alliance between the Auchincloss and Bouvier lineage and the Kennedy's new-found wealth—a convenient marriage of the bride's social respectability with the lofty political ambitions of the groom.

Save for her father's failure to be at her side (he had had too much to drink and was disinvited at the last minute by the bride's mother), the wedding was the event of the season. But the crushing throngs of well-wishers, the fanfare, and the publicity Joe Kennedy had so carefully orchestrated were a far cry from the sort of restrained, genteel occasion the Auchinclosses—and Jackie herself—had envisioned.

Soon the strain of public life became evident. "In the days before her marriage to the Senator, Jackie appeared to be carefree and gay, with a ready smile," recalls Mary Barelli Gallagher, who was Jackie's personal secretary. "But as I got to know her in her Georgetown home, I discovered that her manner was really reserved and introverted—rather living within herself than enjoying having people around her." Only after their daughter, Caroline, was born on November 27, 1957, allaying fears that Jackie was unable to bear children, did the presidential aspirant's wife find a measure of contentment—in the traditional role of mother.

Jack Kennedy's bid for the White House failed to curb Jackie's fervent desire for privacy and peace. She confided to family and friends that she disliked politics, and only reluctantly joined her husband on the campaign trail—a path well worn by a battery of Jack's siblings and their spouses. On one occasion soon after Jack won the presidential election, when a pesky supporter showed up in front of the couple's townhouse, Jackie gave him a copy of her husband's farewell speech to the Senate. When Jack brought home former President Truman, the future First Lady poked her head in briefly to say, "Hello, Mr. President," and then disappeared to resume her tasks.

At times the couple's marriage seemed more like a test of endurance. The rivalries between Jack's rough-and-tumble sisters and his bride, whom Eunice, Pat, and Jean deemed too independent and overly precious, became legend. And there were the Kennedy men's eternally wandering eyes. In spite of it all, Jackie, who was blessed with an aristocratic sense of duty, maintained her composure and, in the end, carried out her obligations with dignity and style.

"The Irish finally made it to Newport," sums up one guest who had attended the September 12, 1953, wedding of Jacqueline Lee Bouvier and Senator John Fitzgerald Kennedy. With publicity staged by the groom's father, the society event of the year caused the worst traffic jam in Newport history.

RIGHT: *The 750 guests jammed into St. Mary's Roman Catholic Church in Newport, Rhode Island, didn't seem to notice the absence of Jackie's father (he was "indisposed," and she was escorted down the aisle at the last minute by her stepfather, Hugh Auchincloss) during the traditional wedding ceremony, which was officiated by Archbishop Cushing of Boston and topped off with an apostolic blessing from Pope Pius XII.*

RIGHT: *Deferring to her fiancé, the bride wore an "old-fashioned" wedding dress that most found lovely but which one critic derided as "an attrocious mass of tissue silk taffeta." The woman whose chic, modern style would later keep her at the top of the Best Dressed List for over thirty years would rarely bow to anyone again in matters of fashion.*

Although Jackie and her mother had originally envisioned a small, private affair, they eventually capitulated to the Kennedys' designs for a grander event. The wedding reception at Hammersmith Farm, the summer home of the bride's stepfather, featured the music of Meyer Davis's orchestra and included enough food and champagne for 1,200 milling guests (many of whom were reporters and cameramen invited by Joe Kennedy). "The Kennedys arrived like Patton's tanks," remembers one of the groomsmen at the wedding. "I felt sorry for Jack. Unlike the rest of the Kennedys, he and his brother Robert were rather shy, and I think they were somewhat embarrassed by all the fuss Ambassador Kennedy made."

Uncommon Grace

RIGHT AND BELOW: *Feasting on an elaborate bridal meal—circa 1953—of fruit cup, creamed chicken, and ice cream sculpted to resemble roses, the newlyweds were toasted by a number of guests, including the groom's brother Robert, right, before cutting the wedding cake, below. Despite Jackie's stepbrother Gore Vidal's claim that the marriage was "an eighteenth-century affair—a practical union on both sides," Jackie, by all accounts, was deeply in love with her husband.*

OPPOSITE PAGE: *After tossing her bouquet of pink and white spray orchids, Jackie changed into a gray Chanel suit and departed with her husband for a two-week honeymoon in Acapulco. Once in Mexico, she wrote a long and touching letter to her father, assuring him that, in her mind, it would always be he who had walked her down the aisle. . .*

RIGHT: *Despite his energetic and youthful appearance, Jack Kennedy had been a sickly child and suffered from a host of maladies as an adult. In December of 1954, he almost died after undergoing complicated back surgery for an injury he had sustained in the South Pacific during World War II. Jackie, who had already suffered the first of three unsuccessful pregnancies, would later describe this period to friends as the blackest moment in her marriage.*

OPPOSITE PAGE: *"Politics was sort of my enemy, and we had no home life whatsoever," Jackie once rued about the early years of her marriage. Seeing her husband off on yet another campaign trip in June of 1957, the Senator's wife would have to face the sudden death of her father, who had been suffering from a liver ailment, a month later. The birth of her daughter, Caroline, in November would finally end six years of uncertainty and much unhappiness for the young Washington couple.*

With a new home on N Street in Georgetown and the birth of Caroline Bouvier Kennedy, whom her father nicknamed "Buttons," Jackie had at last found a sense of security and purpose. A natural mother, she preferred to spend time painting for her daughter and composing amusing limericks for her husband than beating the campaign trail with the rambunctious Kennedys. Nevertheless, at Jack's urging, she allowed cameramen to trail her in Washington and Hyannis Port for the sake of a little pre-Democratic Convention campaign publicity in 1959.

Uncommon Grace

LEFT AND OPPOSITE PAGE: *Once the 1960 Presidential campaign got into full swing, Jackie rallied to give her husband her full support. In October of that year, seven months pregnant with John, Jr., Jackie typed away on a weekly column called "Campaign Wife" for the Democratic National Committee, left, and endured an exciting but exhausting ticker-tape parade in New York City, opposite.*

LEFT: *According to Clark Clifford, who was a friend and the Kennedys' lawyer long before the White House, "Jackie did not seem to fit in well with the Kennedys in the early years. She was drawn to the aesthetic and social rather than to politics or sports, and strains seriously threatened the marriage. But once the quest for the Presidency began in earnest, Jackie involved herself heavily, eventually earning respect and credit from the entire family."*

RIGHT: *Once she jumped into the fray, according to her long-time friend, historian Arthur Schlesinger, Jr., Jacqueline Kennedy took to her new political life more easily than her Newport friends expected. "She came to like politicians and their free and easy talk, and she came rather to like campaigning. She and Senator Kennedy seemed the embodiment of youth and daring in a nation ruled by tired old men."*

PAGES 46-47: *Jacqueline Kennedy, surrounded by Senator Jackson, chairman of the Democratic National Party, and Senator Mansfield of Montana, watched the historic September 26, 1960, televised debate between her husband and Vice President Richard Nixon at the offices of the Democratic Advisory Council in Washington. Youthful and relaxed, Kennedy outshone his rival on camera and beat him at the polls a little over a month later.*

Uncommon Grace

Hope had a new name: it was John F. Kennedy. Glamour a new face: that of Jackie. Together, the 35th President of the United States and the President's wife (she loathed the horsey-sounding moniker "First Lady") embodied the energy and élan of America at a time when "America" meant strength, heroism, and progress.

At thirty-one, Jackie assumed the role relinquished by Mamie Eisenhower. At the historic January 20, 1961, inauguration, where poet Robert Frost came to deliver his commemorative verse, the world was transfixed by the elegance of the new President's wife. Perhaps it was the sharp contrast between Jackie and her predecessor that fostered such admiration. Where Mrs. Eisenhower had championed plain, even dowdy looks, Jackie was inimitably chic. Within a scant few televised minutes, women around the globe were drawn to the young Mrs. Kennedy's magnetic style and modern sensibility.

Much to her distaste, the public and the press seemed singlemindedly obsessed with her appearance over the next three years. And they had some reason to be. Copied faithfully by millions, her clothes were largely couture creations. Not that Oleg Cassini, her official designer, was given carte blanche to supply her wardrobe: having been taught to appreciate continental style, Jackie oversaw a network of fashion scouts— among them, her sister, then Princess Lee Radziwill, who would select and purchase the latest fabrics for her from the houses of Dior and Balenciaga in Paris. The fabrics were then stitched into distinctive fashions by Cassini, so that America's First Lady could hardly be accused of not shopping American. At certain times, however, Jackie would have her scouts—women with similar measurements—buy select Parisian garments and sneak them back into her closets.

Hungry hounds among the press corps were soon accusing Jackie of spending $30,000 annually on clothes. "I would have to wear sable underwear to spend that much," she replied. Widely reported, the sarcastic comment all but ended the First Lady's open sessions with the press corps. On another occasion, when she sported a new, bouffant hairstyle, she issued in writing this response to the public's initial consternation over her brave new coiffure: "All the talk over what I wear and how I fix my hair has me amused, but it also puzzles me. What does my hairdo have to do with my husband's ability to be President?" And of course, she was right.

With the help of her secretary, Jackie answered fan mail from around the world. But it was her children, as always, who remained her first priority. Caroline and John were given full run of the White House, and their birthdays were celebrated with children's parties in the private, family quarters of the Executive Mansion.

In the public arena, one of Jackie's more lasting contributions was the unprecedented sophistication she introduced to official White House functions. Inviting the members of her husband's cabinet to meet the likes of Igor Stravinsky and Carl Sandburg—transforming White House dinners from hitherto dour functions into elegant galas—she put her love of history and culture on the national agenda and made all Americans a little more cultivated in the process. Her love for the arts also manifested itself in the refurbishment of the White House, perhaps her most lasting achievement. During her first official visit to the Executive Mansion as the guest of Mrs. Eisenhower, Jackie observed that the place was so "dark and dreary" that it almost sent her away "with a crying jag." She thus set out to change its appearance and mood.

An unabashed Francophile, Jackie originally wanted much of the new interior scheme to be 18th-century French. But after careful consideration and in deference to historical correctness, she eventually called in the noted American interior design firm of Parish Hadley to help her weave her magic. The result was a presidential residence as wholly American and stately as the occupants themselves.

Was there ever a more attractive couple? The young leaders of "The New Frontier" radiated glamour during a weekend respite in 1963 at Glen Ora, their 400-acre rented estate in Middleburg, Virginia.

THIS PAGE AND OPPOSITE PAGE: *On a bitter cold January 20, 1961, the old guard gave way to the new, as John Fitzgerald Kennedy, symbolically discarding his hat and overcoat, was sworn into office as the 35th President of the United States. Surrounded by no fewer than eight past and future First Ladies, "society girl" Jacqueline Kennedy had yet to win over the great American public—except in terms of fashion. When she accidentally dented the top of her famous pillbox hat during the ride down Pennsylvania Avenue, Seventh Avenue—and women around the country— enthusiastically copied her mistake.*

OPPOSITE PAGE: *Despite all the talk of marital discord, the Kennedys genuinely appeared to enjoy each other's company at public events such as this State dinner at the White House in 1962. "They had little time to chat during the day," recalls former White House social secretary Letitia Baldridge, "and they often took moments at official functions to get in some personal discussions. The President would always instinctively touch the microphones on these occasions to make sure they weren't on."*

THIS PAGE: *Shimmering in Oleg Cassini-designed white organza, the wife of the President-elect was escorted by Frank Sinatra, right, to the Hollywood-style pre-inaugural festivities staged by the singer to help pay off the Kennedy campaign debt. Eschewing her husband's taste for such unsophisticated fare, the First Lady soon hosted elegant evenings with the likes of Pablo Casals, Rudolph Nureyev, and Carl Sandburg. In January of 1962, she and the President welcomed composer Igor Stravinsky and his wife, above, at the south entrance of the White House.*

ABOVE:

After only four months in the White House, Jacqueline Kennedy finally won over every American—not to mention 50 million Frenchmen—during the Kennedys' legendary state visit to Paris. While the press and public focused on the exquisite Givenchy creations the First Lady wore to official functions such as the magical state dinner at Versailles (at which she suggestively donned a diamond tiara), Mrs. Kennedy focused on de Gaulle's cultural minister, André Malraux. "Malraux viewed culture as the modern universal language and saw a new humanism in daily appreciation of art," according to First Lady historian Carl Sferrazza Anthony. "Jacqueline Kennedy then and there made it her ambition to translate this rather abstract notion into a quality of American life. She later quietly tried to install a cultural department within the U.S. government. Unfortunately, Dallas demolished her plan."

OPPOSITE PAGE:

Although her husband failed to charm Nikita Khruschev in Vienna, the next stop on the Kennedys' tour, Jackie demonstrated remarkable grace under pressure at a luncheon in honor of the Russian premier's wife (right background). As Letitia Baldridge recalls: "When the deafening shouts of 'Jack-ie! Jack-ie!' outside the palace began to make Mme. (Nina) Khruschev noticeably uncomfortable, Jackie at once took her gently by the arm and led her to a window. She held up Mme. Khruschev's hand for just a second. The crowd loved it and now began to cry, 'Jack-ie! Nin-a!' It was almost as if they were obeying Jackie's request for courtesy to be shown to her fellow guest. It was an unpublicized—but nonetheless unforgettable—demonstration of Jackie's innate diplomacy and tact."

Uncommon Grace

Although the First Lady's plans for a government cultural department were derailed by her husband's assassination
(he had been carrying the necessary papers to review on that fateful day, she once told writer Carl Sferrazza Anthony), her restoration
of the White House was a lasting achievement. "Everything looked like it came from B. Altman," she had said when she first visited
"that dreary Maison Blanche" after the 1960 election. A little over a year later, she proudly displayed her efforts during her celebrated televised
tour. Albert Hadley, who along with the indomitable Sister Parish, had helped Mrs. Kennedy with the refurbishment of the Executive
Mansion, remembers being instantly impressed with the 32-year-old First Lady's formidable knowledge of history—not to
mention the sheer force of her will. "She knew exactly what she wanted. With a mere whisper of a voice and a smile,
she had people lined to donate the best furniture and paintings."

Uncommon Grace

As a teenage American history buff, Carl Sferrazza Anthony, who years later would write First Ladies: The Saga of the Presidents' Wives and Their Power, once noticed Jacqueline Onassis at a Forest Hills tennis match. "Nobody was talking to her, so I approached her and began to ask her some obscure questions about the White House restoration. She listened, amused, for about fifteen seconds and then, despite having left the White House some fifteen years earlier, smilingly corrected me by instantly recalling that she had put the Hannibal clock on the east side of the Green Room, not in the East Room. Then I asked her about Grace Coolidge's portrait in the Red Room and Lincoln's armchair and Van Buren's bust and the Hoovers' Irish linen. She responded with incredible attention to detail, then graciously asked questions about me . . . . Mrs. Kennedy possessed an exceptional aesthetic sensiblity. In this regard, hers was the most imaginative mind in the White House since Mr. Jefferson's."

Uncommon Grace

  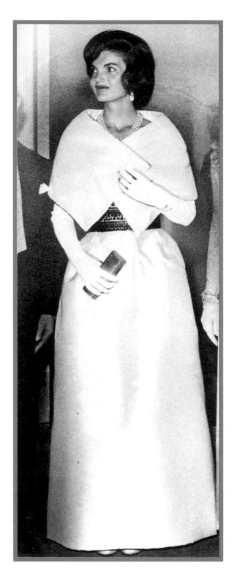

Despite her more substantive accomplishments, the stylish First Lady was quickly dubbed the "First Lady of Fashion"
by the New York fashion press, who voted her to the top of the Best Dressed List her very first year in the White House. Although
she was obliged to wear American designs by Oleg Cassini and others, the clothes were often thinly disguised imitations of originals by
Givenchy, her favorite French couturier. Summing up her appeal during that era, the dean of American fashion, Bill Blass, notes:
"Mrs. Kennedy's youth and good looks made everything she wore instantly appealing—and she was always impeccably turned out.
The clothes she favored were really quite simple and adaptable, and millions of women were able to follow suit.
Of course, her natural grace and mystique could not be duplicated."

Uncommon Grace

THIS PAGE AND FOLLOWING PAGES:
*Jacqueline Kennedy was so popular following her trip to Paris in 1961 that the American public soon allowed their "princess"
to act like one—and get away with it. Announcing her intention in the fall of 1961 to go on a private tour of India and Pakistan with her
sister, the real-life Princess Radziwill, during a period in which she would miss not only Thanksgiving but both of her children's birthdays,
the First Lady was eventually convinced by horrified Presidential advisers to postpone her travels until the following spring. Later, the
reports of lavish receptions and gala evenings spent with maharajas and potentates did little to tarnish the reputation of the
President's wife, whose subsequent unescorted jaunts to Palm Beach, Italy, and Greece went similarly unnoticed.*

Uncommon Grace

LEFT AND OPPOSITE PAGE: *During a three-week vacation in August of 1962 at her sister's 900-year-old villa in Ravello, Italy, Jackie, accompanied by her daughter, Caroline, Lee, and Lee's son, Anthony, thrilled the locals (but not the Secret Service) when they paid a surprise visit to a public beach, left. When photographs of the First Lady swimming with Italian billionaire and fellow housemate Gianni Agnelli appeared in print, John Kennedy wired a telegram: "A little more Caroline and less Agnelli." Mother and daughter returned to Newport, opposite, in time to spend Labor Day weekend with the President and Jackie's mother at Hammersmith Farm.*

PRECEDING PAGES: *Escaping the tedium in Washington and, later, New York, Jackie relished weekends in the horse country of Virginia with friends such as Bunny Mellon, Eve Fout, and C. Z. Guest. "When Jackie came to visit, we were always the first ones up in the morning chomping at the bit, eager to get in the saddle for a full day of hunting," recalls Guest. "Fox hunting meant more to us than any glitzy party. Jackie rode a lovely spotted horse called Rufus, and I hunted my good-looking champion pinto called Harlequin. Jackie and I were quite the pair, galloping across the Virginia countryside on our Indian ponies. Many, many days, we were the last to come in after hours of hunting, all the other hunt members long gone."*

ABOVE:

"My first fight was to fight for a sane life for my babies and their father," Jacqueline Kennedy had once remarked about her life in Washington. A doting mother, she and John, Jr., spied the official welcoming ceremonies for Algerian Premier Ahmed Ben Bella from the Rose Garden in October of 1962, above, left, and attended a ceremony honoring astronaut Gordon Cooper the following spring, above, right. "I was more taken, over time, with Mrs. Kennedy's tireless devotion to her children than with her obvious talents as a political wife and public figure," remembers photographer Stanley Tretick, who covered Jackie in the White House and for years afterward.

OPPOSITE PAGE:

According to former White House social secretary Letitia Baldridge, "Jackie's most effective weapon in raising Jack's spirits when the nation's affairs were going badly was a surprise visit to his office with the children." The First Lady made sure Caroline and John-John had free run of the White House, and pictures of them romping about the Oval Office with the President entranced the nation.

THIS PAGE: *Jacqueline Kennedy's clothes and ever-changing hairstyles so dominated the press about her that the First Lady once demanded in exasperation, "What does my hairdo have to do with my husband's ability to be President?" Created by Parisian hairdresser Alexandre during Mrs. Kennedy's 1961 trip to Paris and later perfected by Kenneth, who jetted down to Washington from New York, the high bouffant the President's wife sported at a state dinner in 1963 for King Hussein II of Morocco, right, and the "upswept" style she had worn to greet the President of Honduras the previous year, below, caused millions of cans of hairspray to be sold and sparked two of the signature looks of the sixties.*

OPPOSITE PAGE: *Once asked if she would make any sacrifices if her husband were elected President, the future First Lady had replied pithily, "Yes, I'll wear hats." By the time she greeted Ethiopian emperor Haile Selassie in October of 1963, Jackie had made the pillbox hat a fashion staple and had helped put a struggling young New York milliner named Halston on the map.*

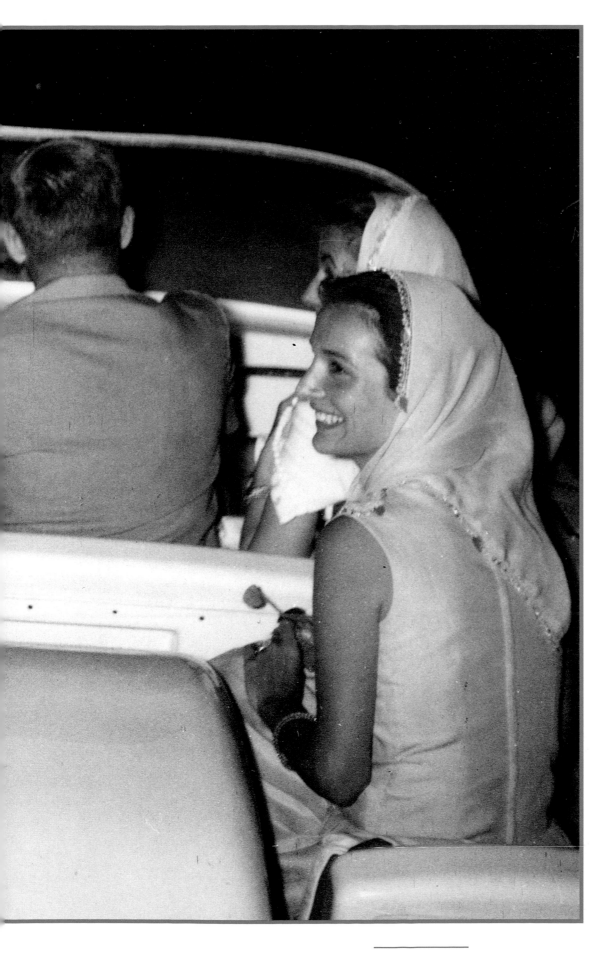

After the death of the First Lady's infant son, Patrick, in August of 1963, Aristotle Onassis invited a depressed Jackie and her sister, Lee, whom the Greek shipping tycoon had dated briefly, to join him onboard his yacht, the "Christina," for a Mediterranean holiday. Aware of the political embarrassment his presence might cause, Onassis offered to stay behind in Athens, but the First Lady objected: "I could not accept his generous hospitality and then not let him come along." Approaching his private island of Skorpios for the first time, Jackie murmured, "Ari, it's lovely. Simply lovely." Her host responded, "This is nothing. I am going to build a copy of the Cretan Palace of Knossos up there, and it will have 180 rooms!" The rest is history. Jackie returned to Washington and in a few weeks accompanied her husband to Dallas. In 1968, she would become Mrs. Aristotle Onassis.

Few would have guessed that a day which began with glorious weather and thunderous cheer would end so tragically. How could a life so brimming with promise and vitality be so savagely taken? At half past noon on November 22, 1963, three gunshots struck the open motorcade that carried the President and Mrs. Kennedy through Dallas's Dealey Plaza. John Kennedy's head jerked back; the assassin's bullets had found their target, and the blood from the mortally wounded young President stained the First Lady's immaculate pink knit suit.

As the limousine sped toward Parkland Memorial Hospital, Jackie cradled her dying husband, a man whose vision had galvanized the nation. John F. Kennedy was pronounced dead later that afternoon. He was forty-six, and she all of thirty-four.

For most of the return trip to Washington, Jackie sat next to the bronze casket in the rear of Air Force One. Her pastel suit was caked with the blood of her slain husband, but she had refused to change her clothes and instead stood instinctively before the cameras as a grim reminder of the powerful force with which the shocking tragedy spilled over to touch the lives of all who admired John Kennedy. The image of her, and that hour, that day in November were etched in the minds of a nation of mourners. And while the assassination triggered near-global paralysis, Jackie recognized that she must transcend her grief; it was she who must tend to the shocked and wounded nation, and it was she who must secure her dead husband his rightful place in history.

Upon her return to the White House, Jackie ordered detailed accounts of President Lincoln's funeral. The mass, at her request, was held at the modest St. Matthew's Cathedral. Following the service, Jackie, flanked by her two young children, emerged from the church to the sound of "Hail to the Chief." Her long, fixed gaze and stately carriage became an example of dignity in the face of grief. Amid muted drum rolls, a riderless horse trod languorously behind the coffin, which was mounted atop the gun caisson that had carried Franklin Delano Roosevelt to his grave eighteen years earlier. The cortège that followed included hundreds of foreign dignitaries.

Jackie had prevailed over a number of Kennedys who wished the burial to be in Massachusetts. The President's final resting place, his widow believed, belonged on a hilltop in Arlington National Cemetery overlooking the rows of graves of other fallen Americans who had served their country.

Perhaps the most indelible image in modern history is one of three-year-old John-John saluting the American flag shrouding his father's casket. This haunting scene, too, was engineered by Jackie. A fortnight later, she gently told historian Theodore White that she had come up with a name for her husband's White House years: "Camelot."

On the sunbaked Dallas afternoon of November 22, 1963, three shots ended the brief life of John Fitzgerald Kennedy and stunned the world. Jacqueline Kennedy would write a year later: "So now he is a legend when he would have preferred to be a man." By then, the President's widow had become a legend herself.

Accompanying the body of her slain husband on Air Force One en route to Washington, Jacqueline Kennedy watched solemnly as Lyndon Johnson took the Oath of Office. "Oh, Mrs. Kennedy, we never even wanted to be Vice President," Mrs. Johnson had said, "and now it's come to this." Confused by shock or, perhaps, intuitively securing the moment's place in history, the President's widow startled her entourage by refusing to change out of her bloodstained suit. "I want them to see what they have done," she insisted.

Upon her arrival at Andrews Air Force Base outside Washington, the former First Lady was joined by a numbed Robert Kennedy, who would accompany her and the slain President to Bethesda Naval Hospital. Buoyed by what she would later describe as "sudden superhuman powers," the President's widow immediately instructed her Chief of Protocol, Angier Biddle Duke, to "find out how Lincoln was buried." Following a sleepless night at a White House suddenly filled with friends and family, she asked a six-year-old Caroline the next morning to write a letter to her father. It said simply: "Dear Daddy, We're all going to miss you. Daddy, I love you very much. Caroline."

The President's funeral on November 25, attended by dignitaries and heads of state and televised around the world, was orchestrated with extraordinary precision by the President's widow for maximum effect. Although theatrical in its flourishes, the muffled drums, riderless horse, and eternal flame all seemed to work. Even more dramatic was the former First Lady's controversial decision to make the funeral procession on foot—almost unheard of in English-speaking countries. Jacqueline Kennedy prevailed, and her instincts, of course, were right.

OPPOSITE PAGE AND ABOVE, LEFT:

A mixture of incredible drama (a three-year-old John, Jr., saluting his father's casket) and simplicity (the Mass cards, simple pieces of paper handed out to dignitaries such as Charles de Gaulle, said only: "Dear God, please take care of Your servant, John Fitzgerald Kennedy"), the funeral organized so swiftly and efficiently by the slain President's wife bound a nation that easily could have slipped into chaos. If for nothing else, her heroic performance that day would confer upon Jacqueline Kennedy immortality for all time.

ABOVE, RIGHT:

In January of 1964, the President's widow went on television to thank over 800,000 people who had written to her following her husband's death. Dignified but still visibly shaken, the former First Lady announced plans to erect a Kennedy Library. Fifteen years later, in 1979, Jacqueline Kennedy Onassis would attend the opening ceremonies of the John F. Kennedy Memorial Library in Boston.

On June 5, 1968, an assassin's bullet struck down Bobby Kennedy, who had been a pillar of support for Jackie during her years of grief following her husband's assassination, and who himself had been waging a promising presidential campaign. Jackie panicked. "If they're killing Kennedys, my kids are number-one targets," she said the day after Bobby's funeral. "I want to get out of this country."

She sensed an urgent need to escape the recurring sorrow and, perhaps, the hubris that had sent Jack and Bobby to early graves. After all, the two elder Kennedy siblings, Joe, Jr., and Kathleen, had also met with premature deaths in the 1940s. Coincidentally, since her 1964 move from Washington to New York, where she had purchased an elegant fifteen-room apartment overlooking Central Park, she had been courted by a number of high-profile and wealthy men. None, however, was as rich or famous as Aristotle Onassis. Although the billionaire Greek shipper had long expressed a romantic interest in Jackie and actually had proposed the unthinkable—marriage—now, with Bobby's death, the idea seemed palatable.

For the widow, who was struggling to make ends meet on her relatively stingy stipends from the Kennedy family and the U.S. government, finally realized that only a Midas such as Onassis could provide the safety and comfort she and her children craved. Self-made and charismatic, Onassis (or "Ari," to his intimates) was also a bon vivant; a combination of old Joe Kennedy and Black Jack Bouvier, both of whom Jackie respected and adored.

On October 20, 1968, Jackie became Mrs. Onassis—with Rose Kennedy's blessing. Teddy, the last surviving Kennedy brother, had negotiated a prenuptial agreement that won the bride three million dollars upon the exchange of marital vows. Caroline and John-John each became the beneficiary of a one-million-dollar trust Onassis set up for them. "She'll get whatever she needs," Ari assured Teddy.

It was a promise that the billionaire, who had longed for a trophy wife, would later regret. Like her father, Jackie had a taste for luxury. She frequented many of the world's purveyors of luxury goods, patronizing Cartier, Van Cleef & Arpels, Chanel, Tiffany, Harry Winston, and Dior, among others. She had traveled quite a bit following Jack Kennedy's death, but now she traveled in grand style, breezing into one exclusive resort only to jet out to another the very next day. The $30,000 monthly allowance from her new husband was often exhausted by the receipts from a single shopping spree.

The press, having manned battle stations from the time the marriage began, now launched an all-out assault. First they implied that the former First Lady had betrayed Jack by remarrying, and now they accused her of taking advantage of Ari. "Sure, Jackie made a few mistakes during her second marriage," a friend once said. "But Ari also exacted from her great tolls," she continued, referring to the insults and humiliation the ailing billionaire heaped upon his wife during his last days. Never a bargain shopper, Jackie knew the price of a marriage-for-money—and she paid it with the sanctified, if unrealistic, status that the public had bestowed upon her.

When Aristotle Onassis died in March 1975, Jackie was given a lump sum of $26 million after some legal jousting with his daughter, Christina. Yet in spite of their arduous relationship, Jackie's public appreciation of her second husband never waivered. "I shall be forever grateful for the generosity, in spirit as in tangible support, Mr. Onassis has shown me," she once stated. "The warmth and affection he gave to my children were rare and irreplaceable."

Jacqueline Kennedy was still the martyred heroine of Camelot when she arrived in Hyannis Port in May of 1964 on what would have been her husband's 47th birthday. By the end of the decade, she would be known simply—and disparagingly—as "Jackie O."

Commemorating the forty-seventh anniversary of President Kennedy's birth, his widow and members of the Kennedy family attended a Mass on May 29, 1964, at St. Matthew's Cathedral in Washington, above, and a service at Arlington National Cemetery, opposite, where John, Jr., placed his father's PT-109 tie clasp on the President's grave. Although the former First Lady rose to the occasion with typical dignity, her friends and family had been increasingly worried about her state of mind. "Jackie called me at home one evening soon after the funeral and asked me for some personal advice," recalls former Presidential adviser Clark Clifford. "We started on the most mundane subject. Gradually, she began talking, at first calmly and then emotionally, about her husband and his Presidency. I felt an unutterable loneliness descending on her. I offered whatever help and solace I could, but there was an unreachable gulf between us, imposed by events. Worlds were closing around her." In the fall of 1964, Jacqueline Kennedy, urged by friends, left Washington—and its bad memories—for the welcome anonymity of New York City.

Having emerged as a paragon following her husband's funeral, Jacqueline Kennedy could never have hoped to live up to the public's unreasonable expectations of her. By 1966, she was hardly trying. In the first six months of that year alone, she skiied in Sun Valley, Idaho, and Gstaad, Switzerland, shopped and partied in Rome, waterskiied at the seaside villa of Italian billionaire Gianni Agnelli, opposite, rode horses at the cattle ranch of industrialist Miguel Carcano in Cordoba, Argentina, attended the Spring Fair in Seville, Spain, and then spent seven weeks "vacationing" in Hawaii, followed by another week in Newport. The jet-setting President's widow roused the most criticism during her trip to Seville. There she stole the spotlight from a visibly unamused Princess Grace of Monaco at a Red Cross gala, above, left, enthusiastically attended a couple of bloody bullfights, and then, in a particularly extravagant gesture, donned a traditional Andalusian riding habit to parade a white stallion around the Seville fairgrounds, above, right.

In June of 1967, Jackie and her children embarked on a six-week "sentimental journey" to Ireland that included a meeting
with President Eamon de Valera, horseback riding at the Waterford estate of her Bernardsville, New Jersey, neighbors, the Murray
McDonnells, and a visit to the late President's ancestral home in Dunganstown, where Caroline and John-John were presented with two
kittens by their Kennedy relatives, above. In November, the former First Lady would fuel rumors of a romance with her recently widowed
friend, David Ormsby-Gore (Lord Harlech), when she asked him to accompany her on a two-week tour of Cambodia and Thailand.

Uncommon Grace

Jetting to Cambodia in November of 1967, America's "Best Dressed Woman" made a three-day pit stop in Rome, paying a call on one of her favorite designers, Valentino. By the time they strolled together on Capri in 1969, the couturier had earned the nickname "King of Italian Fashion" thanks to the patronage of the former First Lady, whose late-sixties "casual chic" style was being copied by millions. "She was always a great inspiration for my work," Valentino recalls. "She had this inner quality to make the simplest dress, the oldest pair of slacks elegant. Her way to wear a scarf, a pair of sunglasses—to go barefoot or wear a tiara—was completely natural . . . she knew by instinct."

RIGHT: *On June 6, 1968, the unthinkable happened again: Robert Kennedy was assassinated in Los Angeles while campaigning for the Presidency. Two days later, his brother's widow, accompanied by her sister, Lee, and her two children, steeled herself for a funeral Mass in St. Patrick's Cathedral in New York City. They later boarded the 21-car funeral train for the burial at Arlington National Cemetery outside Washington.*

RIGHT AND OPPOSITE PAGE: *The eyes of the world were again focused on Jacqueline Kennedy, as she prayed at the gravesites of her husband and brother-in-law in Arlington, Virginia. "After Dallas, Robert Kennedy became the protective element in Jacqueline's life,"* notes author and historian Arthur Schlesinger, Jr. *"She was proud of his opposition to the war in Vietnam, but hated it when he decided to run for President. 'They will do to him what they did to Jack,' she told me in March of 1968. In June, 'they' did as she predicted. Three months later, she married Aristotle Onassis."*

"If they're killing Kennedys, my children are number-one targets," Jacqueline Kennedy had lamented the day after Robert Kennedy's funeral. "I want to get out of this country." The thirty-nine-year-old President's widow did just that and shocked the world on October 20, 1968, when she married the froglike 5'5", sixty-two-year-old Aristotle Onassis in a small ceremony on the Greek tycoon's private island of Skorpios. The American public's brutal reaction to their martyred heroine's remarriage was best summed up by a New York Newsday headline announcing the event: "WHY DID JACKIE MARRY ARI? THERE ARE OVER A BILLION REASONS."

THIS PAGE:

At last fallen from her pedestal, the new Mrs. Onassis—rechristened "Jackie O"—was now scourged by the press, who took vicious delight in divulging the terms of the prenuptial contract Onassis had coughed up to secure his new trophy wife: $3 million outright, a $1 million trust for each of her children, a $30,000 monthly allowance, and $200,000 for each year of her life in the event of a divorce. Although she plainly enjoyed reveling in some of the Onassian luxury, Jackie had always enjoyed the company of older, charismatic men. Despite their separate perches, the couple was still enjoying a long honeymoon, according to friends, when photographer Ron Galella caught them watching a parade from Jackie's Fifth Avenue apartment in June of 1969.

Uncommon Grace

Following the tragic death of his only son, Alexander, in a plane crash in January of 1973, Aristotle Onassis began to increasingly resent his wife's extravagant spending, referring to her as "the supertanker," and Jackie, for her part, was growing bored with the disco-hopping and endless rounds of late-night parties her husband so adored. By the time they were photographed leaving a Paris dinner party in October of that year, they were leading mostly separate lives. Later questioned about his liaison with opera diva Maria Callas, the Greek billionaire offered: "Jackie is a little bird. She can do exactly as she pleases— visit fashion shows and travel and go out with friends to the theater or anyplace. And I, of course, will do exactly as I please."

ABOVE AND OPPOSITE PAGE:

Jackie flew to Skorpios on March 18, 1975 above, to attend the funeral of her second husband, who had died suddenly in Paris three days earlier. She had spent a summer on the island during happier times with sister Lee, opposite, but her visits had been infrequent since her estrangement from Onassis. "Jackie helped make Skorpios, which was rather neglected until her arrival, an Eden," remembers society columnist Aileen "Suzy" Mehle. "Ari, a fun-loving bear of a man, strangely resented her for it. Love had flown, and nothing she could do was right. The master may have had his fill of her, but his staff thought she was heaven-sent. After Ari died, I visited the island, and the maid who looked after me asked, 'Do you know Mrs. Onassis?' When I said that I did, she said, 'Will you please tell her that all of us here on Skorpios love her very much and miss her? We wished that she could be here forever.'" The twice-widowed former First Lady, who, after wrangling with Onassis's daughter, Christina, walked away with $26 million, would never visit Skorpios again.

Uncommon Grace

THIS PAGE: *During her years married to Onassis, Jackie was increasingly hounded by photographers, who no longer showed her the deference she had been accustomed to in the past. When her nemesis, Ron Galella (pictured at right), nearly caused John, Jr., to crash one day as he rode his bicycle in Central Park, an irate Jackie sued—and won. No longer able to come within twenty-five feet of the former First Lady and thirty feet of her children, Galella at least had the satisfaction of costing his favorite subject $275,000 in legal fees.*

OPPOSITE PAGE: *Ron Galella captured the essence of Jacqueline Onassis's singular style in a photograph taken in 1971 that was to become his most celebrated. Summing up her timeless appeal during that era, fashion authority Eleanor Lambert notes: "Mrs. Onassis can best be credited with promoting a new sense of urban chic. She was never overdressed or overbejeweled, and she made wearing pants in the city—not just at resorts—look marvelous and modern. A legion of conservative women followed her lead."*

At age forty-five, after almost three decades in the limelight, the world's most famous woman settled into a life more mundane than most would have imagined. No longer a politician's wife or the spouse of a famous tycoon, Jackie, in 1975, was determined to live the rest of her years in peace and privacy, as she had craved. Now, with her newly inherited wealth and her children young adults, she began pursuing those goals that had long eluded her.

Always a bibliophile, she became an editor at the publishing house Doubleday after a brief stint at Viking Press. Armed with her legendary charm and celebrity status, Jackie helped secure for her employer works from renowned figures in show business, the arts, and society. Among her star recruits were singer Carly Simon, performer Michael Jackson, and Gelsey Kirkland, the prima ballerina.

Having abandoned the frantic social schedule of the Onassis years, she could often be spotted at a favorite Manhattan restaurant—like "21," La Grenouille, or The Four Seasons—leisurely lunching with her authors by day. At night she would venture out only to attend events that benefitted causes dear to her—notably the Municipal Art Society, which, with her help, blocked the destruction of New York City's historic Grand Central Station.

According to the old society adage, the first time, a woman marries for love, the second time for security and comfort, and the third for companionship. Although she did not remarry, in the late 1970s Jackie seemed to have found, in Belgian-born Maurice Tempelsman, a source of happiness she had little known. A brilliant diamond merchant and financier, Tempelsman had been separated from his wife. Perhaps it was his continental charm and powerful intellect that attracted her. Surely, it was his complete devotion that bound them. With his guidance, and in several years' time, she saw the $26 million left by Onassis swell into a fortune of well over $100 million.

There were, of course, her children. Caroline, by the mid-1980s, had matured into a highly intelligent woman whose implacable will many compared to her mother's, and in 1986, Jackie happily presided over her Hyannis Port wedding to Edwin Schlossberg. The young couple in time gave Jackie three grandchildren—Rose, Tatiana, and John—who were their grandmother's endless source of joy. John, Jr., who inherited the Bouvier good looks and his parents' charisma, was Jackie's principal focus. She steered him through thick and thick—nudging him into a respectable career in law and out of a series of romances she knew could only bring him heartache. Success in this crucial area of her life now assured, she passed on a bit of her hard-earned wisdom to neophyte First Lady Hillary Rodham Clinton: "Remember," Jackie offered, "if you bungle raising your children, I don't think whatever else you do matters."

For a woman who religiously ran and swam, practiced yoga, and watched her diet, the diagnosis in early 1994 of non-Hodgkins lymphoma must have come as a severe blow. Yet she fought the disease for months with characteristic valor, continuing to work uncomplainingly until the final days. Then, on May 19, a melancholic procession that included old knights of Camelot and longtime friends filed into her Fifth Avenue apartment; by then a nation was keeping an around-the-clock vigil, disbelieving that the end of someone forever young in our collective consciousness was fast approaching.

The next morning, John, Jr., issued the following statement to a tearful America: "Last night at 10:15, my mother passed on. She was surrounded by her friends and her family and the books and the people and the things that she loved. And she did it her own way and on her own terms, and we all feel lucky for that, and now she's in God's hands."

Indeed, Jacqueline Bouvier Kennedy Onassis had always done it her own way and on her own terms. Although the road she traveled was sometimes treacherous, by adhering to her instincts and persevering as a role model in the public eye, she showed each of us what it means to live with uncommon grace and die with dignity.

Financially secure after her marriage to Onassis, Jackie spent the last two decades of her life quietly —tending to her children, working, and enjoying her hard-won independence. But she never forgot history. In May of 1992, she attended an awards ceremony at the John F. Kennedy Memorial Library in Boston on what would have been the President's 75th birthday.

Janet Norton Lee Bouvier
Auchincloss, though seldom
seen in public, joined her
daughter for the 1975 graduation of granddaughter Caroline
from the Concord Academy in
Concord, Massachusetts. She
had sold most of Hammersmith
Farm, her Newport property,
around the time of her husband's death in 1976 and
would begin to suffer from
Alzheimer's Disease in the
1980s. Later, Jackie would set
up a trust fund for her mother,
so that she could live out her
final years in comfort.

Even during her marriage to Onassis, Jackie had never severed her ties to the Kennedy family. She could often
be counted on to attend official ceremonies honoring the memory of her first husband and enjoyed the occasional Kennedy-clan get-together.
At this 1980 clambake in Hyannis Port, she joined some 50 other family members, including Eunice Shriver, Ted Kennedy,
and Ted's daughter, Kara, to celebrate matriarch Rose's 90th birthday.

Uncommon Grace

During the last twenty years of her life, Jacqueline Onassis increasingly lent her support to a number of worthy causes.
In 1972, she attended the opening ceremonies of the John F. Kennedy Center for the Performing Arts in Washington with conductor-
composer Leonard Bernstein, top. Closer to home, she joined the board of the Municipal Art Society in New York. "It is hard to imagine how
the great battles to save St. Bart's [Church], or Central Park from a giant shadow [of an office tower proposed at Columbus Circle], or the
landmark law itself, could have been won without Jackie's quiet voice," notes the society's current chairman, Stephen Swid. "She thought to
make New York the civilized and magical place she always knew it could be." Jackie scored her biggest preservation triumph at a 1975
news conference in which she convinced city officials not to destroy historic Grand Central Station. Joined afterwards by architect
Philip Johnson, New York City Cultural Affairs Commissioner Bess Myerson, and Mayor Ed Koch, bottom, Jackie celebrated
a landmark preservation victory and one of her greatest accomplishments as a private citizen.

Dividing her time between family, carefully chosen fund-raising projects, and work (she would join the staff of Viking Press in 1975),
the widow of Aristotle Onassis disappointed "Jackie watchers" by making only rare public appearances, at events such as a book-signing party
(with Gloria Steinem in 1984, top), and the annual Robert F. Kennedy Pro-Celebrity Tennis Tournament in Forest Hills (with Howard Cosell,
Ethel Kennedy, and Robert F. Kennedy, Jr., in 1976, bottom). More elusive than ever, Jackie seemed intent, at last, on leading a
"normal" life. "At the time, no one considered Jackie as a separate human being, as the person she was and would have been, whether or not she
had married a future President or Aristotle Onassis," recalls her long-time friend, Ms. magazine founder Gloria Steinem. "When she was alone
again after Onassis's death, the speculation about her future plans only seemed split in two. Would she become a Kennedy again (that is, more
political, American, and serious) or remain an Onassis (more social, international, and simply rich)? What no one predicted was her return to
the publishing world she had entered briefly after college—to the kind of job she could have had years ago, completely on her own. And that's
exactly what she did . . . Her example poses interesting questions for each of us: given the options of using Kennedy power or living the interna-
tional lifestyle of an Onassis, how many of us would have chosen to return to our own talents and less spectacular careers? In the long run,
her insistence on work that was her own may be more helpful to other women than any use of the conventional power she declined."

RIGHT AND OPPOSITE PAGE:
Mixing a little glamour with good works, Jacqueline Onassis, accompanied by artist Bill Walton and Eunice and Sargent Shriver, lent her magnetic presence to a Valentino fashion show in June of 1976 to benefit the Special Olympics. Always the center of attention wherever she went, Jackie had long ago learnt how to shrug off the glare of publicity. "One of the remarkable things about her was how she bore the stress, the nuisance of being a public figure," recalls her long-time friend, Paris Review editor George Plimpton. "Perhaps because she was so young—it is astonishing to think that she became First Lady at the age of thirty-one—she was able to deal with celebrity with such grace, and indeed humor. Bill Barry, a fellow editor at Doubleday, once described traveling with her on the shuttle to Washington. The two had arrived late, just before the gates closed, and on the plane had to walk down the aisle to the last two seats left, far in the back. Not only did the passsengers gawk at her as she went, but once seated, the plane moving down the runway, they continued to turn and peer at her over the headrests. At this point, Bill told me, Jackie turned, smiled, and in that throaty way of hers whispered to him, 'Bill, they all know you!'"

LEFT AND OPPOSITE PAGE: *In 1975, at the suggestion of her spokesperson, Nancy Tuckerman, Jackie accepted a $10,000-a-year job in the publishing industry as a consulting editor for Viking Press, picking up the career she had abandoned a quarter of a century earlier. Amid media speculation about her salary and how long her "whim" would last, Jackie, according to a colleague, "quietly went to editorial meetings, suggested ideas and authors, got her own coffee, made her own phone calls, waited at the Xerox machine to do her own copying, and worked on a variety of book projects [including* The Firebird, *which she helped acquire, left]." . . . "Those first days couldn't have been easy," continues the colleague, "especially since she had to make herself vulnerable to a whole group of New York publishing professionals with a 'show me' attitude and an inclination to gossip." Jackie's involvement at Viking (she would move to Doubleday in 1978) reached its peak with the 1977 publication of* In the Russian Style, *a lavish coffee-table volume designed by Bryan Holme, opposite, and edited by Mrs. Onassis.*

Jacqueline Kennedy Onassis never forgot the legacy of her first husband. In June of 1977, she attended the groundbreaking ceremony for the John F. Kennedy Memorial Library in Boston, gamely removing the first shovelful of dirt and proclaiming the event "his most fitting memorial." Joined by her two children, Jackie would attend the opening ceremonies two years later. "She never talked about the past or the President," remembers Albert Hadley, who had helped the former First Lady refurbish the White House. "In her apartment in New York, the only indication of those times was an important bureau plat she had placed prominently in her drawing room that displayed a number of the President's papers and favorite objects. It was a simple—but dramatic—testimonial."

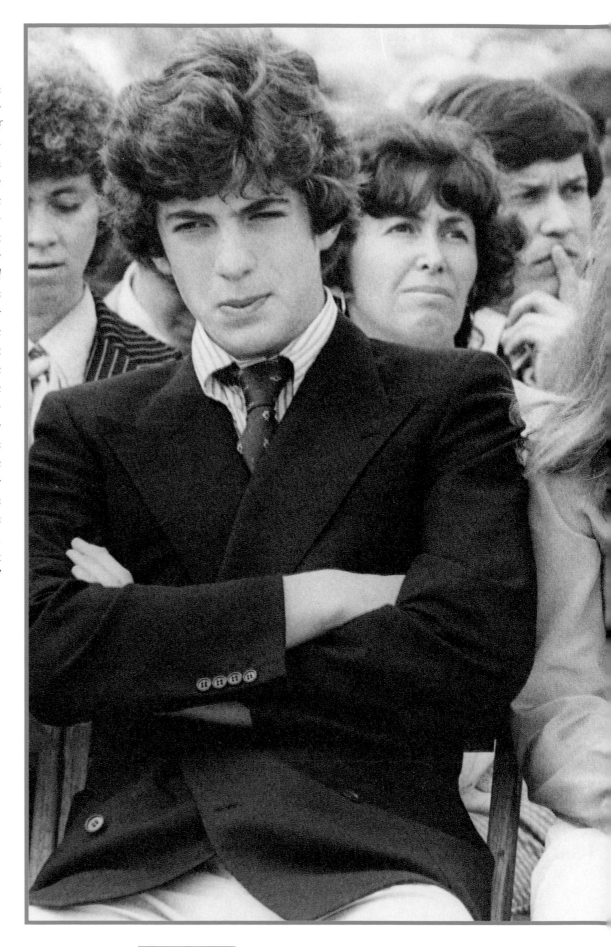

THIS PAGE AND OPPOSITE PAGE: *The year 1986 was a particularly happy one for the rarely-seen-in-public but still glamorous 57-year-old working mother, whose greatest accomplishment, she felt, was that her children had grown up relatively unscathed by the weight of the Kennedy legacy. In April, escorted by her son, left, who had inherited her father's devastating good looks, she journeyed to Hyannis Port for the wedding of Maria Shriver and Arnold Schwarzenegger, then returned in July, below, left, to watch Caroline marry Edwin Schlossberg, a conceptual artist thirteen years her senior. Following her daughter's ceremony, she was escorted from the church on the arm of Ted Kennedy, opposite, who later toasted Jackie at the reception as that "extraordinary, gallant woman, Jack's only love."*

Uncommon Grace

SOME FLASHES OF JACKIE: *I was sitting on a blanket next to her at one of George Plimpton's July Fourth fireworks parties in the late seventies in Wainscott or East Hampton, and I mentioned that an English writer friend we had in common, Charlie Maclean, was going to be in town that week—his uncle, Hugh Fraser, was one of her sometime escorts. In those days Charlie's dress code was blue blazers, black chinos, and blue-black sunglasses. She looked toward me through those big Jackie Onassis shades she never took off, and asked me with great curiosity and almost concern, "Why does he always wear those dark glasses? Is there something wrong with his eyes or is it just an affectation?" A couple of minutes later Heyward Isham passed by our blanket and she threw out, "I used to have a crush on him."*

Another time I was walking my 200-pound Newfoundland in Central Park and ran into her. She remarked, "You must be so nice to have a dog like that," and I said, "Didn't Bobby Kennedy have one?" She said, "His name was Brumus."

My friend the late Charles Addams, the cartoonist, took her out quite a bit in the years following the assassination. He was invited to her mother and stepfather's place, Hammersmith Farm, in Newport, for the weekend. She gave him a tour of the property, pointing out this, that, and the other thing, and when she left to go inside for a moment, her mother asked Addams, "Why was Jackie whispering?" He shrugged and told her, "Well, she always whispers," and the mother said, "I must ask her why." Addams and Jackie dated to the point where she once asked him, "What if we got married—what would we talk about? Your latest cartoon?" That's a cartoon in itself.

Addams was also a great friend of Garbo, who surprised him one day by asking if she could meet Jackie. He invited them both to dinner at his penthouse apartment on West 54th Street. Garbo arrived early and she was so nervous she got loaded on vodka, then panicked and left five minutes before Jackie got there.

When I signed a contract a couple of years ago with Doubleday, the company she worked for, to write the biography of producer Leland Hayward, whom she had known, I wrote asking her for her recollections of him. She had Nancy Tuckerman call me to say that she really didn't have any stories. Some time later I saw her at a party—she asked how the book was going and said she was sorry that she hadn't had anything to contribute. But when, like any good journalist who's finally got his quarry cornered, I primed her with specific questions, it turned out she remembered a lot more than she thought—all of it characteristically expressed. I asked her why she'd worn white to Hayward's wake in 1971. She answered, inscrutably: "He deserved it."

—STEVEN M. L. ARONSON

LEFT: *Jackie worked for fifteen years at Doubleday, editing dozens of mostly lavish coffee-table volumes and using her name and influence to aggressively court celebrities as diverse as Greta Garbo, Carly Simon, Gelsey Kirkland, and Barbara Walters. Eventually promoted to full editor, the elusive Mrs. Onassis helped her publisher cut a deal in 1984 with the even more elusive Michael Jackson, who had agreed to publish his memoirs if Jackie came on board as editor. The following year, in the singer's office at his Encino, California, estate, Jackie, accompanied by her assistant, Shaye Areheart, worked with the project's designer, J.C. Suarès, left, to choose photographs for the book (to be titled Moonwalk) from Jackson's personal collection.*

OPPOSITE PAGE: *The subject of endless romantic rumors following the death of Aristotle Onassis, Jackie was at one time or another linked to everyone from William Paley and Ted Kennedy to Prince Rainier and architect I. M. Pei, a long-time friend whom she accompanied to China in 1982. Pei at one point took Jackie to visit his family home in Suzhou (where she met his granddaughter Alyssa, opposite). "Old Chinese houses have carvings on the walls—calligraphy, sayings," recalls the architect. "She was particularly taken with two panels. One said 'See Fragrance,' the other 'Read Paintings.' Of course, she felt this was fascinating. After we returned, she painted a picture for me in the Chinese style, with black ink. It said 'See Fragrance' and 'Read Paintings.' She was a lady of great sensitivity."*

ABOVE AND LEFT:
"My wonderful little house,"
Jackie called the 19-room
Cape Cod-style retreat she had
built on 425 acres of prime
waterfront property in
Martha's Vineyard. Spending
her summer weekends there in
the company of Maurice Tempelsman, a diamond merchant
who had become her long-time
companion, Jackie welcomed
Bill and Hillary Clinton for a
day of sailing in August of
1993, above. In October, the
new First Family joined the former First Lady (shown with
Joseph P. Kennedy, III, and
John, Jr., left) for the rededica-
tion of the JFK Memorial
Library in Boston. It would be
her last public appearance.

"Her grandchildren were bringing new joy to her life," Ted Kennedy said of Jackie, who loved to spend time in Central Park with Caroline's three children, Rose, left and below, Tatiana, left, and John Bouvier Kennedy Schlossberg, known as "Jack." In the 65th year of her life, the twice-widowed former First Lady, who had led such a remarkable life and who seemed content, at last, to move gracefully into old age, suddenly discovered she had cancer. It would be the last hurdle in a life filled with obstacles and one which she faced with characteristic dignity.

After she was diagnosed with non-Hodgkins lymphoma in January of 1994, Jackie refused to give up her daily outings in Central Park, where she was photographed with her constant companion, Maurice Tempelsman, just four days before she died. She told her long-time friend Arthur Schlesinger, Jr., "I feel it is a kind of hubris. I have always been proud of keeping so fit. I swim, and I jog, and I do my push-ups, and walk around the reservoir—and now this suddenly happens." "She was laughing when she said it," he notes. "She seemed cheery and hopeful, perhaps to keep up the spirits of her friends." Jacqueline Lee Bouvier Kennedy Onassis died on May 19, 1994.

Uncommon Grace

In the end, the woman known simply as "Jackie" belonged to the public—and it was the public who came to pay their respects outside her apartment building the day after she died. A week earlier, seventy-nine-year-old Alberto Arroyo, a fellow jogging enthusiast and a fixture around the Central Park Reservoir where Jackie had liked to run, stopped to chat with her as she sat quietly watching the other runners go by. Which country, out of all of her travels, he asked her, did she like best. The woman who had twenty-five years earlier once felt compelled to leave all of the tragedies of the sixties behind and "get out of the country," thought for a second and then answered simply: "What's wrong with America?"

LEFT AND OPPOSITE PAGE: On May 23, 1994, John and Caroline Kennedy, left, watched as their mother's casket was carried from Manhattan's St. Ignatius Loyola Church, where Jacqueline Lee Bouvier had been baptized sixty-four years earlier. Later, at Arlington National Cemetery, opposite, Jacqueline Kennedy Onassis was at last laid to rest beside her first husband, her infant son Patrick— and the eternal flame.

"No one else looked like her, spoke like her, wrote like her . . . no one we knew ever had a better sense of self . . . Jackie was too young to be a widow in 1963, and too young to die now. She was a part of our family and part of our hearts for forty wonderful and unforgettable years, and she will never really leave us."

—SENATOR EDWARD M. KENNEDY

"May all the world remember Jackie with respect and even pride. May they face death, when it comes, with integrity and composure and trust in God, just as she did. May God give her peace and joy in Heaven for all eternity."

—SARGENT SHRIVER

"Jacqueline Kennedy Onassis was an extraordinary combination of resilience and utter grace. She rose beyond what she was asked to do, and—in the end—never lost sight of who she was inherently."

—ALBERT HADLEY

"Perhaps against her wishes, Mrs. Kennedy was the most glamorous woman America ever produced. She became the symbol of the perfect American, an example to millions and millions of women. She was a wonderful mother and cared deeply for her close friends. She had a tremendous sense of privacy, although she was never able to escape the public eye. In the end, whatever she did she always did in the most gracious and loving manner."

—OSCAR DE LA RENTA

"Every time I saw her, I had to pinch myself to remember that this was one of the great heroines of history, for in my eyes she was just a human being . . . . Beneath her elegance lay a great fund of culture. Her gift of hospitality was rooted in anticonformism, and the wit she wielded sprang from an open mind. Her simplicity in all things masked the incomparable richness of her personality. She was straightforward and loyal in friendship, which for me made her even more appealing . . . . But most of all she was a woman, a creature of absolute mystery and fascination to the last."

—HRH PRINCE MICHAEL OF GREECE

"America will miss her strong character, her enigmatic smile, her natural elegance, her style, her kindness to all people in need, that magical whisper of a voice, and that God-given grace to be able to stand up in dignity and silence against all the vicissitudes that life brought to her. Jackie never explained—and I will miss my friend."

—CAROLINA HERRERA

"The last time I saw Jackie, in November 1993, we reminisced about the wonderful times we had fox hunting together. There was no one else who came to visit me in Virginia who had the staying power to stay up late into the night and still get up early to be on a horse by seven a.m. . . . . Jackie and I had such a good time together—she was not only an elegant lady but a great sport. I loved her, I admired her, and I will miss her so much."

—C. Z. GUEST

"Jackie was a great benefactress of New York. Surely by example she has left a kind of legacy within all of us who love where we live—to extend our efforts, perhaps even more than we ever thought we were capable of, to make our towns, our cities—our homes— better and more exhilarating places in which to live."

—GEORGE PLIMPTON

"Jackie's admiration and respect for artists and their work was abiding and infectious. Her love of the arts was impassioned and informed by broad knowledge and great taste. She became for many people a kind of symbol of what is best about American culture."

—ASHTON HAWKINS

"Jacqueline Kennedy Onassis was a model of courage and dignity for all Americans and all the world. More than any other woman of her time, she captivated our nation with her intelligence, elegance and grace . . . . Even in the face of impossible tragedy, she carried the grief of her family and our entire nation with a calm power that somehow reassured all the rest of us."

—PRESIDENT BILL CLINTON

"If she taught us anything it was to know the meaning of responsibility—to one's family and to one's community. Her great gift of grace and style and dignity and heroism is an example that will live through the ages."

—HILLARY RODHAM CLINTON

OPPOSITE PAGE: *Jacqueline Kennedy and John Fitzgerald Kennedy, Jr., in the Reception Room of the White House, November 30, 1962.*

*Thank you thank you dear J.C.
It is always such a joy to work with you —
Until our next book — and love to Nina*

Jackie

A note to the author, 1986.